MY first
IOO
FOOD
we eat

fruits

apple

pear

watermelon

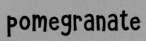
pomegranate

strawberry

peach

banana

pineapple

blackberry

avocado

blueberry

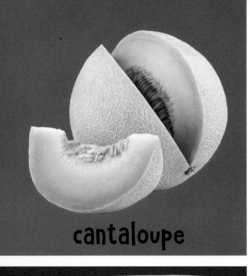

cantaloupe

sapodilla

grapes

papaya

guava

kiwi

dragon fruit

grapefruit

custard apple

green apple

coconut

raspberry

cherry

apricot

starfruit

fig

cape
gooseberry

plum

tomato

cranberry

lychee

vegetables

green bell pepper

potato

radish

turnip

onion

carrot

lettuce

cauliflower

zucchini

broccoli

celery

cucumber

brussels sprout

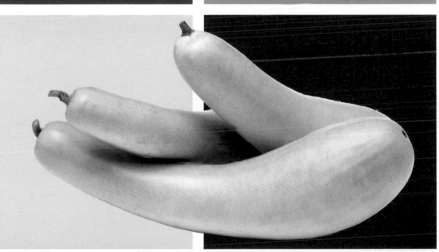

eggplant

green pea

asparagus

sweet potato

okra

yam

drumstick

ginger

green
bean

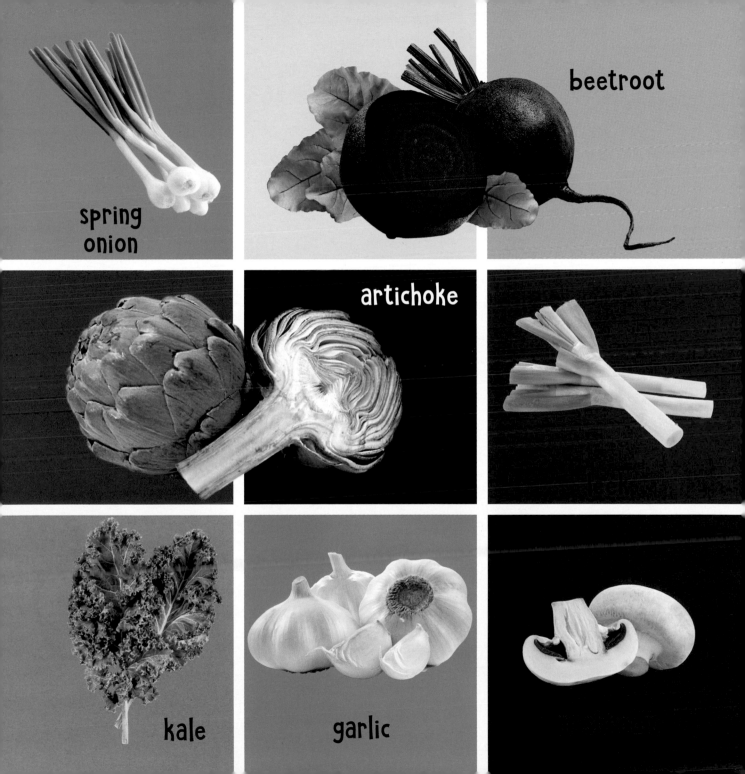

spring
onion

beetroot

artichoke

kale

garlic

food

cornflakes

juice

fruit salad

milk

sushi

trail mix

soup

chicken

honey

cereal bar

waffle

taco

fish

cheese

spaghetti

rice

cookie

chocolate
pudding

muffin

 cake

 dumpling

 cereal

 yogurt

pancake

 pasta

pizza

popcorn

chocolate

ice cream

macaroni

tofu